WILDERNESS RESCUE PILOT

BY PATRICK PERISH

Are you ready to take it to the extreme?
Torque books thrust you into the action-packed world
of sports, vehicles, mystery, and adventure. These books
may include dirt, smoke, fire, and dangerous stunts.
WARNING: read at your own risk.

Library of Congress Cataloging-in-Publication Data

Perish, Patrick, author.
  Wilderness Rescue Pilot / by Patrick Perish.
    pages cm. -- (Torque. Dangerous jobs)
  Includes bibliographical references and index.
  Summary: "Engaging images accompany information about wilderness rescue pilots. The combination
of high-interest subject matter and light text is intended for students in grades 3 through 7"-- Provided by
publisher.
  Audience: Ages 7-12.
ISBN 978-1-62617-199-2 (hardcover : alk. paper)
 1. Search and rescue operations--Juvenile literature. 2. Bush flying--Juvenile literature. 3. Bush pilots--
Juvenile literature. 4. Aeronautics--Relief service--Juvenile literature. I. Title. II. Series: Dangerous jobs
(Minneapolis, Minn.)
  TL553.8.P47 2015
  363.34'81--dc23
                                    2014036731

This edition first published in 2015 by Bellwether Media, Inc.

Printed in the United States of America, North Mankato, MN.

TABLE OF CONTENTS

CHAPTER 1
LOST!

Two climbers are lost in the mountains. To find them, a search and rescue team takes to the skies. The pilot flies low over the area where the climbers were last seen. Soon the **spotter** locates them among large rocks. Slowly, the pilot moves in close. She is careful to avoid nearby trees. Then strong winds blow in suddenly.

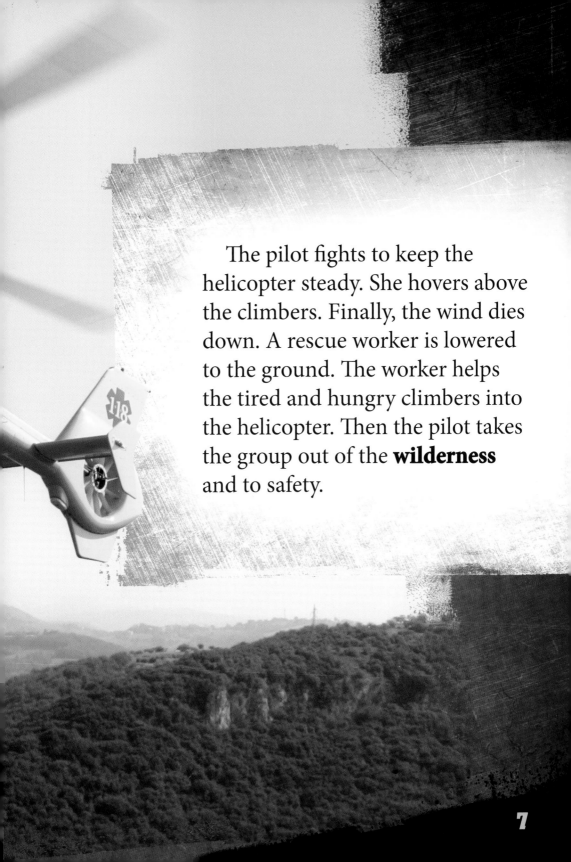

The pilot fights to keep the helicopter steady. She hovers above the climbers. Finally, the wind dies down. A rescue worker is lowered to the ground. The worker helps the tired and hungry climbers into the helicopter. Then the pilot takes the group out of the **wilderness** and to safety.

CHAPTER 2
WILDERNESS RESCUE PILOTS

Wilderness rescue pilots fly airplanes and helicopters to **remote** locations. They go where other emergency response teams cannot. They rescue people from mountains, forests, and other hard-to-reach areas. Pilots take airplanes for fast searches over large areas. Helicopters are more **maneuverable**. Pilots use them for rescue work in tight spaces.

A Wet Landing

Some rescue pilots fly floatplanes. These planes land and take off on water. In some areas, lakes are the only clear place to land.

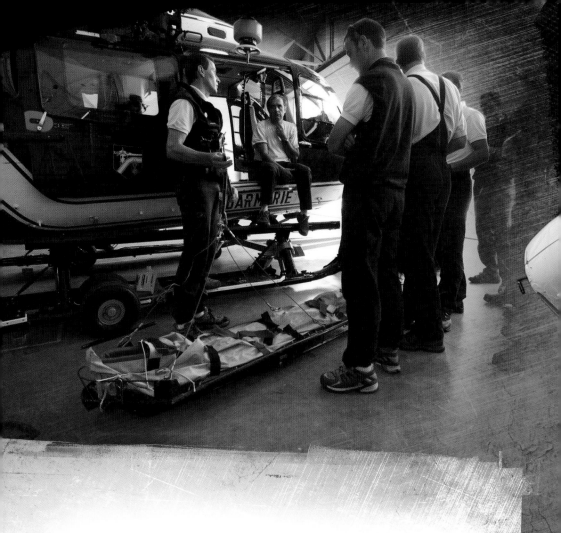

Rescue pilots go through a lot of training before they get their **licenses**. First they train with **instructors**. They take classes on **navigation** and aircraft **maintenance**. Then pilots practice flying. They train for hundreds of hours before they can join rescue crews. Pilots also learn survival skills and **first aid** in case of emergencies.

landing skid

Rescue pilots master many skills. They need to be able to hover in a helicopter. They often take off and land with limited room. Sometimes rescue pilots have no place to land. They might need to rest one **landing skid** on the edge of a cliff to drop rescue workers off.

Canines Coming!

Pilots sometimes fly rescue teams with search dogs into wilderness areas. The dogs help search for missing people.

Special gear helps rescue pilots get their job done safely. Pilots use **GPS** to navigate. They use a **hoist** to lower and raise rescue workers. **Night-vision goggles** help some pilots fly in the dark. All pilots need to have good communication with their team on the ground. They use radios to stay in touch.

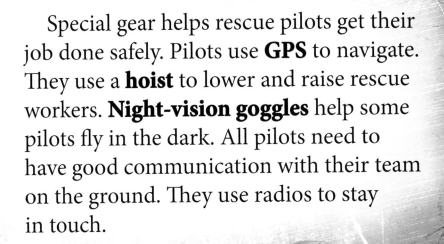

Valuable Vests

Some pilots wear survival vests. These are packed with food, water, and supplies in case the pilots need to spend a night in the wilderness.

hoist

DANGER!

Wilderness rescue pilots usually fly with little notice. They sometimes have to fly at night. This makes it harder to see trees, cliffs, or telephone wires. Hitting these can cause the pilots to crash. Rescues often happen during dangerous weather. Storms can form quickly. Pilots risk crashing in heavy winds, rain, or snow.

Landing and taking off in tight spaces is very dangerous. One wrong move can lead to an accident. Pilots often must fly long distances. Long flights can be exhausting. Tired pilots are more at risk for making mistakes.

Wilderness rescue pilots face danger every time they are called out. Even so, pilots are determined to save lives. They are willing to make risky flights to help people in need.

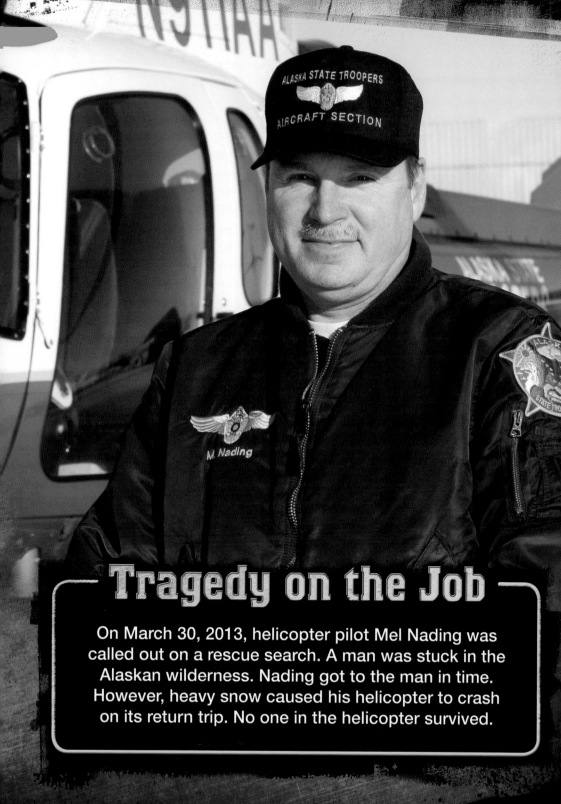

Tragedy on the Job

On March 30, 2013, helicopter pilot Mel Nading was called out on a rescue search. A man was stuck in the Alaskan wilderness. Nading got to the man in time. However, heavy snow caused his helicopter to crash on its return trip. No one in the helicopter survived.

Glossary

first aid—emergency medical care given to a sick or injured person before he or she reaches a hospital

GPS—a system that helps pilots know where they are; GPS stands for global positioning system.

hoist—a device on a helicopter used for lifting and lowering people

instructors—teachers

landing skid—one piece of the long, flat landing gear of a helicopter

licenses—official permission to fly a plane or helicopter

maintenance—the practice of keeping something in good working condition

maneuverable—able to be carefully steered

navigation—finding one's way in unfamiliar terrain

night-vision goggles—special sets of glasses that allow pilots to see at night

remote—far away from populated areas

spotter—a person who rides with a pilot during search and rescue missions to be a lookout

wilderness—undeveloped land that is home to plants and animals

To Learn More

AT THE LIBRARY

Gordon, Nick. *Coast Guard Rescue Swimmer*. Minneapolis, Minn.: Bellwether Media, 2013.

Oxlade, Chris. *Mountain Rescue*. Chicago, Ill.: Raintree, 2012.

Rajczak, Kristen. *Rescue Dogs*. New York, N.Y.: Gareth Stevens Pub., 2011.

ON THE WEB

Learning more about wilderness rescue pilots is as easy as 1, 2, 3.

1. Go to www.factsurfer.com.

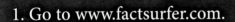

2. Enter "wilderness rescue pilots" into the search box.

3. Click the "Surf" button and you will see a list of related web sites.

With factsurfer.com, finding more information is just a click away.

Index

The images in this book are reproduced through the courtesy of: Chris Crisman/ Corbis, front cover; Roberto Caucino, front cover (small), pp. 18-19; Marka/ SuperStock, pp. 4-5, 6-7, 12; EC Photos, pp. 8-9; John Van Hasselt/ Corbis, pp. 10, 20; ImageBroker/ SuperStock, p. 11; Frank Leonhardt/ Corbis, p. 13; Patrick Baz/ Getty Images, p. 14; Graham Taylor, p. 15; Anze Bizjan, p. 15 (background); mato, pp. 16-17; Lonely, pp. 16-17 (background); Alaska State Troopers/ AP Images, p. 21.